The Vessel of One

*Channeled Messages from Angels,
E.T.'s and Saints*

To Johny

Love [signature]

By

Craig Lefebvre

ISBN: 13:978-0-578-47077-1

Copyright: 2019

Editing by Jill Behme Conaway
Creative Director Johnny Chadziewicz
Technical support Melissa Lefebvre

Book jacket design by Flor Figueroa
Time-Stream Artwork: Amy McNamara

Dedicated to my wife, Melissa.

Thanks for loving my kind of weird.

I am the Mulder to your Scully.

Table of Contents

Introduction:

I am most thankful that I have made it this far in my spiritual life's journey. I also humbly accept that I too have a long way to go on this road of self discovery and spiritual growth moving into the future. Many events, people, teachers, and unique experiences have led me to this moment of writing this book. Looking back in time I started this "interest" in all things paranormal when a childhood friend showed me a book from the library about famous hauntings. This sparked my curiosity. From there, another friend in high school had introduced me to an author named Dan Millman and his book "Way of the Peaceful Warrior". - I cried while reading it. Stories like this made sense to me and were the direction I needed to be going. The second big thing that moved me was while attending college I had learned to meditate from my therapist. Therapist? Yes, I was depressed as a teenager and still do occasionally battle depression in my adult life. I pursued meditation with great enthusiasm after reading a book on OBE's (out of body experiences). After a year of practice, I finally achieved my goal and made a major breakthrough.

While getting my body relaxed as humanly possible (progressive muscle relaxation) I again kept seeing a grey square tunnel each time I would meditate. This was totally frustrating... was it my imagination, or maybe I was stuck somewhere? Why wasn't I having the experience like I was reading about in the book on OBE's? I kept meditating because it helped me feel so much better internally. That was until one day I was going through the gray tunnel and I looked down and saw a bright green baseball field below me. Then suddenly startled, I looked up and saw an Extraterrestrial sitting across from me. Between the two of us was a square hole in the floor. I was on a ship, a UFO if you will. I came back into my body quickly after seeing this. I was in awe.

It was then that the Pleiadians came into my life, or at least I had discovered they were there all along and had been monitoring me from a distance. It wasn't until I began channeling that I had learned they had been with me since birth. But I digress. The meditation practice continued and I kept getting more wild visions, seeing more and more locations that I couldn't even begin to understand. It was messing with my head in a big way and the enormity of the situation was more than I could process. I started reading volumes of books on all matters related to the new age, occult, spirituality, past lives, and many other similar subjects. I couldn't absorb enough information on the subject and still feel that way today. The E.T. phenomenon had become part of my secret life that I could only share with a few select people that I trusted or wouldn't try to commit me to a mental hospital.

While in college I was studying hotel restaurant management. It was after taking those unrealistic career interest tests that schools make you take that stated "this is what you should do for a career". I took it to heart. In college I met Sister Diane Garret who became my tutor and LD counselor. I had been labeled "learning disabled" as a child early on. I'm sure it had nothing to do with the fetal alcohol syndrome or cracking my head open on the pavement after falling off my bike in the second grade. Diane was my savior and helped me talk about the things that I was seeing and the problems I was having in school. In college, depression was my enemy and Diane in her own way helped me navigate through some of it.

After leaving college I went back and got a degree in desktop publishing. Then after a year of working split shift, I went to work for a weekly newspaper selling advertising. While I was working there 9/11 happened. That day I will never forget. My phone rang and it was Diane. She had tracked me down. The first words out of her mouth were "you were right". I had shared my visions of the twin towers collapsing with her on a few occasions, because it just kept coming up. This was a few years prior to the event. I was horrified and yet relieved at the same time to know that the visions were for real, and I wasn't losing my mind, at least not yet... On a personal note my thoughts and prayers continue to go out to all those families who lost their loved ones on 9/11. Commuting in and out of NYC weekly for my day job, I am constantly reminded of that tragic day.

CHAPTER 1

Tuning In

In the Fall of 2017, I had a reading with my cousin-in-law, Michelle Behme, whom is a very talented psychic medium. I have had the good fortune of getting to know her very well on my journey, as there are only so many people you can discuss psychic phenomenon and extraterrestrials without being ridiculed or laughed out of the room. It was among family members like her that I first started passing on messages from our deceased relatives. I don't consider myself to be a medium by any measure. Rather, I consider myself to be a channel. Channeling is more like a stream of thought process opposed to a medium who is conversing for the deceased on the other side of the veil. It is very rare that I throw questions at the source, unless I'm channeling for myself personally. The conversation is mostly one way, while channeling.

During the Fall of 2017 reading with Michelle, I kept getting messages about writing. She stated "I keep seeing you writing, lots of writing" Writing what exactly? "I see you bringing in new information, channeling I think". It was Michelle who suggested that after the reading to sit down and write and see what comes out. I was skeptical to say the very least, that I was going to get something. The following day I went to a bookstore in New York City and bought a wire bound sketch book and a black marker. I just sat there and "tuned in". I doodled for a while, drew shapes and symbols. I did this a few times and then put it aside to pursue other interests, as I didn't get any immediate results.

It was maybe four months later that I was on the train to NYC watching random You Tube videos. One popped up with Lee Carrol channeling Kryon. I had read his 11:11 book back in the 90's and even watched a few videos along the way of his unique channeling work. But, on this one day it just hit me as to how powerful the work he was doing actually was. I decided that I needed to be doing something like that. I needed to have some greater purpose or voice here on Earth. My life needed to matter. Then and there I set out to break through the self imposed wall which held me back. I sat with pen and paper and scratched out a channel. It was nothing great but I had done it. Pushing forward, I kept at it and the messages started coming in. First it was from my Angels. Then the Pleiadians came through and kind of dominated the conversation for a while. After that the channels were a mixed bag of angels, saints, earth elders and others. This is why I ultimately titled a chapter in this book (Everybody in the Pool). It makes me laugh sometimes though, as one evening I came home after returning from a meeting and Freddie Mercury was standing in my kitchen wearing a bright yellow jacket. He was fanatical and pushy about his message being perfect. Another time I was driving home on Valentines Day with some take away sushi when Michael Jackson tried to push a message to me. It was weird, as I was listening to AC/DC really loud and a message about friendships with little boys came through. Stop right there I said! Oh hell no, I am not doing this one. I drew the line there.

Channeling has become my weekly ritual now. A few times a week I'll sit down at the kitchen table after the girls have gone upstairs to do their nightly reading, as they most often do. I'll have my special pen in hand and a sketch pad with no lines. I put on my headphones with something musical to drown out the background noises. My ritual is to say to spirit, "I connect with the highest high, I connect with the goodest good, and I connect with the lightest light." If you're already doing this type of work you'll have realized the great importance of being tapped in to the light while channeling. If not, you will learn the hard way when bad stuff comes through or even worse clings to your energy field. To the uninitiated, don't ever start a practice like this without some sort of guidance from a teacher, or healer. I myself have been doing healing-energy work for over 17 years now and have seen what is out there. If you are not protected, you can get hurt. For example, one day I met a stuck 9/11 soul at Whole Foods in Midtown Manhattan that needed to be crossed over. I set my intention and took the subway down to the 9/11 memorial to do a soul crossing for this stuck soul. On the subway platform a demon-type wraith entity appeared, somehow knowing what I was heading to do and got right up in my face. This is why everyday I use a redundant four layers of protection, as I never know who or what I may bump into.

My background in healing extends from traditional Reiki, to the newer LaHoChi, and also from Energy Medicine. Each of these modalities has it own unique value and belief system. What they all teach though, is to channel energy with good intention in order to help individuals overcome physical pain, mental illness, and to move stuck energies. Also, these modalities at their core are just channeling energy, plain and simple. Learning hands on healing is a good place to start if you have some spiritual inclinations to help others on your journey here. Studying with multiple teachers will also be of great benefit to you as well. In this you will be exposed to different philosophies and learn what resonates with you personally. I've seen firsthand students who follow around just one teacher and act as lapdogs to them. Please don't ever feel tied down to one spiritual practice, as there is no one-all and be-all healing modality. The more you pursue in your spiritual exploration, the more well rounded you will become.

With all that said, now I bring to you a collection of my first year and a half of channeling with some commentary and thoughts attached as well. This is not a book that is to be read in one sitting but rather is one to be read in short intervals. This is so you may reflect and ponder the messages given here. Each one has its own flavor so to speak, as does each source that it came from.

I was struck to find a common thread between all the messages and voices coming through to me. They came with love and a wanting of humanity on the whole to wake up, seize the beautiful opportunity they have in front of them and to grow spiritually as well. No matter what your personal belief and or religious practice may be, you are sure to identify with at least a few of my channels. In essence they all want to help you and to be heard; for I am their vessel.

Note: Each and every channel I do will be both titled and ended with my signature "channeled by Craig". The grammar and writing style will also change from message to message. Each one was rewritten shortly after being received. The fluidity of the thought is much more important than the actual grammar. I end each channel in saying "in service to all and the One" and by One I mean God and all that serves the light. One is the constant theme that will be heard throughout most of all of my channels. Please open your mind and enjoy the journey.

CHAPTER 2

Angels Come Calling

Seven colors of light, words from Gabriel

A possibility exists in all humans who have positive intentions for good. He who is in position to receive God's hand will hold light through their heart. A light of many colors shines for mankind at this point in his existence. Kind words to one another will wash away the stains of greed and harmful energies. Angels sing at the doorsteps of men who give reverence to the One God. Healing takes place when you're open with one another and not disguising or misleading intentions about who you are. Be open to a new potential reality that exists in all our hearts, mankind.

Channeled by Craig
In service to all and the One

For the fallen

A few words on death and our perceived relationship to it. From birth we are taught that we have one life in this Christian culture. It is not so, as Jesus did explain to his most loyal disciples. He himself once abroad in India studied with masters of which he himself was to become. Now because of mans need to control in the darkness you believe something else, something more shallow… But now be informed, for we are the Angels sent to guide you, the truth in the matter. Matter does not cease to exist, it only changes form. You will always exist into eternity. And like a scripted drama the soul agrees to come back again and again as your sisters, brothers, uncles, mothers, and fathers etc. Love and rejoice in one another as to take turns handed down in this 3D reality. Also, just for the record dear humans Jesus ascended with us as other masters have done before him. Love Archangel Michael

Channeled by Craig
In service to all and the One

A message of two, part 1

I am conscious at this very moment looking beneath our feet. Sometimes few things can touch us here in our hearts. As the Earth turns, a heart beats and a system of rhythm is developed. For now humanity has an ability to sing its own song and navigate its own future. Waters move quickly here smoothing away the crises plaguing all humanities future aspects. It isn't easy, nor is it necessarily complicated to understand the golden ratio in and around a humans DNA pattern. Look inside, you've got the wherewithal to now do so as it is your freewill. - Archangel Gabriell

Channeled by Craig
In service to all and the One

A child not yet born

A short story of life and how it is birthed here on planet Earth. First and foremost it is a gift and responsibility to host a soul as parents here. In some instances we are not yet responsible or legally engaged as parents yet when a soul is called through. In these times a soul may volunteer to come through only to be terminated before drawing its first breath of air. This is choice and this is freewill. The soul chooses not by way of design but rather out of sheer will. Or in other instances the garnered soul may get cold feet and back out of the allotted contract. We as humans carry grief, it is of by emotional design, or our energetic matrix if you will. Now in this moment draw in another breath and release your guilt. You are forgiven and this is what you came here to learn. Birth of life as well as loss of life can be a great gift to you, if we choose to see it as such. Don't carry this forward another day, you are forgiven. Life goes on. -Archangel Michael

Channeled by Craig
In service to all and the One

From Archangel Michael

To say a star burns bright is an understatement. A human whisper is all we need to hear to be present and waiting by your side. Protection is offered but not always taken. As is your right it is human free will to accept our hand being offered to you, humanity. A word was spoken once, that word is God. All present in everything and everyone. The new day is here now for humankind to change its attitude in being. This comes without judgement, as it is not our position to do so. You already judge yourselves enough as it is. Put Love into your hearts humanity. Stop the childish bickering and political hatred. This wasn't your purpose in our creation. Just be Love.

Channeled by Craig
In service to all and the One

An Angelic channel for today

A Precious moment lays in front of you. Try to imagine all possibilities available to you all at once. As if time folds in on itself, collapsing to one positive moment, taking away all the negativity. Now realize this infinite possibility is available only when you've opened your heart chakra. A new space is being cleared now for all of us. Hold out your hands in front of your face. Ask for forgiveness and let angelic love flow through you. Now, new Earth welcomes you into 5th density. Why isn't it here already you ask? Have you bothered to look around? Stop staring at the negative which is fighting the Light as we speak. Instead embrace only truth. No more false reality controlled by the Dark. Now accept light from both archangels Michael and Melchizedek. Ask for their assistance daily in order to see past the dark on your planet. Realize and create a new Earth in 5th dimensional reality. Embrace what is your truth. Amen

Channeled by Craig
In service to all and the one

A message from Archangels Melchizedek and Michael

So right off the bat the world is changing. Most people say or can at the very least recognize this situation occurring around them. But to be clear they all don't understand the real change happening to them. At least not yet. When the water washes over them; so many will sit up and finally pay attention. They will say the change is real! Yes, it has always been there, the change that is real. A touch from Source, the Creator. Archangel Michael will bring his fiery blue flame sword but not to protect this time but rather to instill change. Opening up a doorway and entry to changing one's own beliefs. What do you believe anyway? The question you need to be asking one's own self, the question to be concerned about today. As now a new future rapidly approaches you. Will you pray at the last minute? And are you black or white, or so to speak good or bad? What is it you stand for? In recognition for all that exists, we the Angels bow to the Universe as its will is to change. This comes for everyone... not all will be able to see it. Some, like we've said before, are too caught up in their "technology devices" to even hear our whispers. Change is right there for those who are ready. And our hand as always awaits those whose prayers ask for help. -Change, light and the infinite.

Channeled by Craig
In service to the all and to the one

Community and Faith

If I could write these words myself, I very well would have. But I can't, and I'm now able to speak with you all today via channel. I am Lorde Joseph a secular Angel sent here to administer words of hope and faith for the now sometimes faithless. Yes, some of you have awakened to the call, as it has become much lighter even during these most turbulent times.

I would like to start by saying, please be faithful to one another and reward your fellow man with good trust when he bestows on you his good deeds. The holidays are now upon us and it's important to not just share good food and company but also good faith as well. As there are still many here who are faithless and it saddens the heart. Yes, yes it does.

Connect with your fellow men and women and build good community this year. This is what creates good faith indeed. All will prosper at once when good faith is shared in community. The next time you are alone please both reflect and meditate upon these words justly. All is One, for if not then there would be nothing but void in your lives. Keep the faith, amen.

-Lorde Joseph

Channeled by Craig
In service to all and the One

Wisdom from an Angel

Greetings and blessings dearest ones. This is Archangel Michael with words about wisdom. I ask, do you even know or realize the wisdom in your own lives? I am projecting this thought to you all simultaneously who are willing to accept my message of love on this glorious day. I repeat here again; do you know what wisdom even is?

I'll start here again by saying wisdom is truth in the matter of every decision you make for today and tomorrow. It is your highest message to be received in communication with one another. Now I offer you some thoughts; they are mostly positive for change. Let us all put our grief aside, shall we? Let's also take a step back, as it is not that serious and you are all okay. You are all exactly where you agreed to be at this point in time.

So now let's say goodbye to strife, goodbye to grief, and anguish too. Now is now and now is the present moment. The confluence point where you are to say, I begin anew again. I start anew today! All my grief and my ill thoughts are being left behind. You see it is that simple and the choice is yours. The choice is of freewill to exist in a positive time frame. Break free from the bondage of negativity. Let us conclude today's message and say use your wisdom, express your freewill, and choose to be more positive, amen.

Channeled by Craig
In service to all and the One

The Connectedness

I welcome all those who wish to come before me. Be thoughtful in who you are while contemplating this communication today. You may now consider that your energy is your everything and your everything is but one singular point. It is a singular fractal of which the universe is made of. It doesn't need to be any more complicated than that either. There is both a simplicity and a complexity in the oneness. This is giving you and everyone else here a duality.

A broken matrix exists in front of you right now in your immediate time space. A fracture has occurred in this very moment so that you can observe who it is that you really are. Be with that thought for a moment and while you all are collectively sitting in that thought, I want you to reach out to one another with your minds. Yes! At this very moment. Reach out and feel the connectedness of those who are also sitting in this very moment. You are all One, you have chosen to embrace the messages here in the now. Be unified, be allowed to feel one another, as you truly exist outside of the matrix. You are all One. Lets now be in completeness, amen.

-Lorde Metatron

Channeled by Craig
In service to all and the One

From Metatron

In the new dimensional reality no one sits alone. What this means is that we're never alone... Not even for a second. From the moment you are born, your guides, Angels, are a constant presence in your life. You may dismiss them as just aberrations, but trust in God's light. The way-shower is always in your life. As a child you were gifted the imaginary friend, the feeling you knew deep inside to be true. The trust is still there, but are you listening? Or are you a self absorbed person who can't think past yourself? Yes, I called you selfish! It's time you've heard it from me Archangel Metatron. Be prepared to listen once again, as you'll need us very soon. And now we're here watching, waiting to speak with your soul once more. As all of you could use some guidance right before the hour of need, right as the clouds start to gather outside your doorstep. Time to wake up Humanity, time to transcend your reality. A hand is being offered here. We are but a prayer and a whisper away friends.

Channeled by Craig
In service to all and the One

Today's Channeling from Archangel Melchizedeck

This is Melchizedeck the servant of peace once again. Greetings dearest ones, followers of light and way-showers for humanity. A big struggle is going to unite humanity once and for all. Why you ask?! Because from your core beginning this was your greater spiritual purpose here on Earth. Not to hate one another, but to join hands as sisters and brothers, God's true creation. For a moment let soft red light flow down your spinal column... This is love and purpose to share with your home Gaia Mother Earth. Even now at this point in your 3D reality you begin to panic! Silently the energy grows with a moment of manic intensity for you... Those, those who are to be left behind... They will be driven mad by this new higher vibrational frequency. Now this is not what you thought I'd say, questioner? But do believe as I am God's messenger! Now, I see relief in your eyes when I'm close to you. Believe me, the choice is yours it is completely. Either step inside the new dimensional paradigm or cease to exist as the creators right hand. A new day has come, to be reborn unto his image. Be not afraid, as it is I who guide you in the days to come.
-Archangel Melchizedek

Channeled by Craig
In service to all and the One

Words from Archangel Gabriel

Sometimes we look upon you dearest humans with a complete amazement. You are carrying this burden we call separateness. It happens to be by your birthright. You come in as a soul to be born into a physical reality, yes. You agree to forget that which you agreed to forget. Your whole life may be encompassed by a singular thought questioning, why me?

The answer is simply because you are. Be perfect in who you are no matter what your life is about. Life is the gift and forgetting is part of that gift as well. How else would this journey be worth the reward? All that matters, is that you simply are. Nothing else. Be loved as you are, amen.

Channeled by Craig
In service to all and the One

Blood on my hands

There are no wounds which we cannot heal, especially those of the heart. Blessed are those who are in service to the light on this very day. The moment of the One has risen for all to see in the glory of God's creation. The sun will shine hotter as we enter the 4th cycle of Earth's evolution. The pain and suffering will come to an end when those who suffer choose to look through the heart. Feel as it is to feel through your solar plexus. The truest sense comes through your body. Use this to listen instead of your mind. The body is your device to unlock your soul potential here. Do not abuse it. Glory is for all those who accept love into their heart, amen. -Lorde Michael

Channeled by Craig
In service to all and the One

Twilight for mankind

The sun, the Earth, and the moon. These three things work in sequence in order to create a habitable place for both men and women to exist together in perfect unison. We agree that you are not unlike any others across the universe, except for one thing, your emotions, which constitute your morality to be in the flesh and blood of a human body. Your range of emotion is not like that of any other being of embodiment. This is a gift from God's hand of creation. Through this emotional construct you will learn what others can not. The greatest of which will be compassion. But the darker side of man is filled with rage and anger; not something that can be easily contained. But you've eaten the apple of knowledge and through this deed you shall know better. Also mankind must learn to quench this inner flame and rationalize as to why he must control such an emotion like rage.

In this time sequence you are upside down and right side up... the positive in the inverse of all rationality. The tide shifts and you do not know why. At the very least for those who have chosen to remain asleep, the light is now coming through the open doorway. Gods hand welcomes you there. Listen to your emotional body to now feel the broader spectrum of who you really are. Have you yet to explore such things? Let go of the animal instincts and touch the divinity in yourselves. The ONE did not release you all to run amok, but rather so you could remember who you really are.
-Lord Joseph and Gabriel

Channeled by Craig
In service to all and the One

CHAPTER 3

Saint Germain the Violet Flame and More

The Violet Flame

Greetings dearest humans. I am awake and aware, I am you. I am the I am. St. Germain here to give a message of rebirth. First let us begin as I say hello from the other side of the veil. This veil has to be lifted for all to see, for all to consume light. Darkness inhabits your existence in third density. Let's now move past it… the choice is free will. God's gift to humanity, so you may experience yourselves in multiplicity. For if you think it, it is yours. If you believe it, it is yours. The will to create one's own true reality. Now a decision needs to be made on your part. Either heal and work through your human issues or stay sitting in the darkness, where light cannot reach. What do you choose, humanity? The choice is yours.
-St. Germain XOXO

Channeled by Craig
In service to all and the One

Both a channel and personal note for 9/11
9/11 channel for Man

A time transfer occurs each time we have this conversation. We are the elder fathers of planet Earth, both Enoch & Jesus come here to present both a very complex and yet very simple message for man to understand. Wisdom lies in its own corridor of truth. Men seek power and great corruption falls in their laps. Words get spoken at one another and hatred begins to happen. Certain people provoke this madness through the news media outlets. Such as it happens right now at this very moment. If truth occurs it won't be through these so called news outlets. Let men have faith deep in their hearts, for you are not perfect and justly so. A moment's rest occurs today at the 9/11. We hear prayers for men and mourn the loss of human life from our side of the equation. Be at peace, mankind for soon you may be at war with one another again. Stand up for what's right in your own eyes. Stop being sheep to the dark ones controlling the news and media.

Channeled by Craig
In service to all and the One

Note: A special thanks to Diane my college counselor who called me at work on 9/11 and said "You were right." Not only was I able to share my visions of the future and unburden my mind to her but she also introduced me to channeling the Angels. Diane was the first person to channel my angel for me. What I thought was very unique about her channeling, was that she would channel writing with her left hand, which was her non-dominant hand. Writing a channel out is called automatic writing, this is what I do, too. God rest her soul as she is now on the other side.

The Fisherman and Servant

A fish gets caught and then brought to shore for another man to eat. In return currencies are exchanged. Forever it seems to have been your process of doing exchange involving currencies on your planet. We have often spoken through Craig about the process and vibrational frequency of the ONE. It is in your genetics, the frequency of exchange. A process rich in agreement and goodwill for human kind is the exchange of gifts.

Now be both welcoming and accepting of those things that are enrichment to your mortal lives that come without price tags. Recognize those things and each other as being such gifts. Learn to trade things and hand down knowledge just like these words are being handed down to you now. Food for the soul. Your soul experience is why you are here, and if you listen, truly listen, you will be rich beyond belief. So, are you the man buying the fish or are you selling it? Are you being the fool or are you the prophet? Be rich in who you are, not in by what you own, amen.

-Lorde Joseph

Channeled by Craig
In service to all and the One

For Man, some compassion

Compassion is your answer and you didn't even need to ask the question. I am now so far removed from the human suffering that is going on here right now. And I am feeling ashamed that I cannot be there to help all my spiritual children, to learn and to grow as I once did. Now things are different for humans in their individual life experiences. Lots of complexities and nuances exist for you all. Imagine if it were much simpler. I for one would very much like to see humanity put back into their most basic element. Such as God, Family, and Church, food, water, and shelter. This would be just so it could be simpler for you all.

This world you now navigate as individuated souls is being overshadowed by something grave and insidious. We call it ego, for your easy understanding. It is a ruling factor in your

governments and social structures right now. This ego robs you, starves you, and keeps a "lessor class" permanently enslaved to a system that continually oppresses. You could all do well to pay attention to this as it's a reflection of your inner selves. Now learn, listen, grow, and most of all show some compassion for your fellow man. Blessed are those seeking the Lord and Savior, amen.
-Saint Theresa

Channeled by Craig
In service to all and the One

Note: I was feeling very flattered for having been visited by Mother Theresa who insisted that I call her Sister Theresa instead. She also showed up at the 9/11 memorial one day while I was crossing souls over who were stuck there. Very cool to see her just show up and help like she did. What a beautiful soul she is.

Words from St. Yoseff

In the words featured at this conscious moment in thought translation, we offer greetings from far away, and yes to your future selves as well. For you are your own salvation in this moment of time. You are all aspects of the same precipice connection adhering to a future moment yet awaiting to take place. There are thoughts amongst your people today as to who controls these situations sitting before you now. The answer is simply, you. You have a voice don't you? You have God given free will don't you? Can you not figure out a way to coexist with one another? And each time you give in to bad opinions of hate, you let darkness win. Is that what you want? And do you really act as if you live in these beliefs of love and justice? Be noted that judgement shall reign down upon those from heaven, those who have not yet chosen to serve God's will. The will, will be as divine as a newborn baby's glimmer of hope, that very twinkle in its eye. Now judgement comes upon yourselves because you have free will. I know you get angry with God our father who art in heaven when you falter. If you need someone to blame, look into the mirror dear friends. The point today of all this is to say when darkness in the form of a man comes and reigns terror upon you, it is a reflection of yourselves as a whole society. Why do you sit and stair at the TV while atrocities begin to unfold before you? Have you made peace yet with your soul creator? Is it possible you missed the point of all this sitting in your human arrogance? Judgement will come and there are those disciples in my holy flock who won't be in fear. It is time to separate the wheat from the chaff. Be well and look onward.

-Yossef

Channeled by Craig
In service to all and the One

The Virgin Mother

In our words to our heavenly father we respond in good faith to those standing in thoughtful appreciation today. All are blessed who come to the aid of the many. Bring your children before me in both thought and prayer. Such as those who are crippled both mentally and physically. It is both by intention and by my hand that I bring healing to those in need, those who are cast out, and those who have been rejected by society for their maladies.

Bring an offering in my name for those you see upon the streets. Money of coin, food, water, or whatever have you. All those in need are a reflection of your selves. Be blessed all for I bring the mother's healing hand to all who will accept me. Amen, the Blessed Mother Mary.

Channeled by Craig
In service to all and the One

We are as One

Blessings are given unto you my brothers and sisters. This is our highest hour. Our hour of need. This need has yet to be explained for you are all in the same predicament. The circumstances are literally laid out here at your feet. These are the one's made up of your own devices. The world is at a 3D tipping point. Our power on the other side extends well beyond your worldly needs. But it is your own power which you yourself now needs. Deep inside you all, there is a spark. You may have even forgotten that it is even there. That is why we send you these words today.

Take a thoughtful moment if you will and sit still by yourself. Collect your thoughts and then empty your mind. Let the internal dialogue fade away. Here in this space of silence; you may trace back your soul's journey. In this journey you've forgotten those who are in your soul cluster. You grew up with them, went to school with them, and created a physical family unit with them. You all had to agree in one unified thought to create a reality matrix together. For if you were not in agreement this all would fall apart. The matrix would blur.

Now we must share that which we alluded to earlier on in this channel. Each of you now can co-create a new world reality matrix together. This world does not have to stay the same. You do not need to be in agreement with the old outdated archetypes. Especially if they no longer serve you! Now you know what the need really is. It's change, for you all are ONE, amen.
-Lord Joseph, St. Anthony, and Mother Teresa

Channeled by Craig
In service to all and the One

For the child

Oh there are children, poor children, living so impoverished on the streets. I shed many tears and hope and pray that my cause be heard. The church has not listened, as I had once hoped. Poverty could be ended in a day with the redistribution of wealth. There exists the technologies as you know that can very well shift the tide, helping the poorest of the poor. Free will is of God's chosen gift to humanity. Listen all, listen as One. It is your decision to either be conscious or to be a slave to your own greed. Both lust and desire are the cardinal sins separating you from one another. Won't you hear my plea, for your own sake? Be blessed.
-St. Elizabeth

Channeled by Craig
In service to all and the One

In my eyes

I am possibility as so you are and always have been. Listen carefully I tell you, the words are in the mouth of every human and every species throughout the universe. The mouth opens, in come the words and our connection has been made with you. Connecting with spirit can be so simple. What thought creates is amazing. Quantum mechanics cannot yet describe what is actually taking place when we channel messages through Craig. It is possible for you, and as you have the gift, if you so choose to let it in. This is no special talent. It is however pure intention and yet that is all it ever takes to put words to the page.

Parts of the Bible were written in this very way. Does that seem blasphemous to you now? You all possess the ability to listen in on spirit and accept its gifts of creativity. And I declare that you are not all birds locked in cages. Not unless you want to be. Angels hear and they listen intently, for your prayers. Heaven's gates open and accept all who stand for love. So please abolish your hatred for one another. A new day has come and it is simply glorious. Amen.
-Saint Yossef

Channeled by Craig
In service to all and the One

Dancing in the woods

Read more about the rules and regulations that govern this body of people here. Are you independent, left or right perhaps? We say none of this matters in the spectrum held by light. Angels don't stop waiting at heaven's gate because your opinion is inflammatory over your neighbor's view point. Stop seeking reasons for being different and seek those of sameness, like being human. This is Saint Anthony and I've got words to say here as humanity's fists are held in rage over differing opinions. Have you ever heard the story of The Crucible? The meaning in this invocation is most important for your people, America. This country wasn't born or started in darkness but has most certainly befallen to it. Let all your rage subside and connect with one another through each others eyes. See that they are you, see that they are as of each and everyone. Amen, and so it is.

Channeled by Craig
In service to all and the One

Violet Flame:

In service to all that we say in comparable agreement today. In service to the Light. A new road opens today for humanity's sake. A much singular-like crack has appeared on the surface of the said Darkness. It is beginning to erode. Love creates this fracture shattering perceived time. I lift the veil so that humanity catches a glimpse of what is truly real; what is true reality. I am St. Germain, whisper my name and you shall feel my presence be near. The said darkness may run and hide on this day as these words chase it away with an Angel's breath. Who are you in your true cause, humanity? What words should I say to make you take your power back and give true individuation once again? The apple of knowledge was a gift, not a curse as some would infer. The longest road you have taken. Stop your lollygagging and take command of your circumstances. Be individuated but also be as One.

-St. Germain

Channeled by Craig
In service to all and the One

Men in tall hats

A spirit has risen now that the Christmas holiday season arrives for humanity once again. Please take the opportunity to greet one another with common courtesy. Now let's draw you in closer as I tell a spirited story of the past. It was not long ago that most of your peoples attended mass on Sundays. This was not forced control but was considered civil obedience. Now the tides have turned. People are now withdrawing from the so called mass religions and gravitating towards a more personal spirituality. I find this delightful. This is also a good thing as the Catholic church cannot be trusted with your children. The elders of the church have turned a blind eye to the pedophilia! The denial was and always shall be, pure insanity! Darkness can intercede if you do not keep a watchful eye. And I am ashamed of the Pope's dissonance regarding this matter.

Now question why is it that the Vatican is so rich and the biggest real estate owner worldwide? To what purpose does this serve? Greed perhaps? Keep a watchful eye on your children please; I beg of you. Do not trust these men in fancy hats. They are not who they say they are.
-St. Anthony

Channeled by Craig
In service to all and the One

NOTE: I sent this channel via e-mail to the Vatican. They did not reply back, which is not a big surprise.

Thoughts and prayers to see

In a moment you will open your eyes to a new possibility. One which exists throughout time and space. This will be a dipping in of your toes into a new reality (so to speak). One that exists outside of your own. It is like whispers being shared back and forth between two lovers. They are so close that they might not even need to speak. To this end you must look inside to see that which requires your souls presence at this moment in time. In other words, what is your calling? How can you be of help to others? Where will your extra pocket change benefit the poor and needy? Is there compassion that can be shown and positively impact another life? Now as the new blue light arrives here on your planet, an awakening is also happening. Look at those around you... Some will simply blossom and unfold like beautiful petals of a flower. Then others will shrivel up and simply detest life. Their bitterness will be most obvious. Make no mistake about it, for the change is coming and I offer my prayers for you all.

-John the Baptist

Channeled by Craig
In service to all and the One

For all my children

A single star that appeared in the sky to guide those who knew he was coming… to be born, but this time again. What is it to be born again? For you dear humans have not been forsaken. Just as Jesus appeared again in his own flesh and blood, so can you. Assuming you take in faith and believe that there is much more to this human earthly form than you ever could have imagined. Blessed Mother offers her hand. The virgin birth was no accident, but rather a way of proving a point. The light exists in each and everyone of you. Through compassion and caring for others I too came to realize this. It was at my last breath here on earth when I heard heaven speak to me finally. And for all those years I had helped others, I did it in good faith. Plain and simple; I believed. A true believer. Our heavenly father did not forsaken us. The truth is we actually are the FATHER, the Holy Spirit, and all that is combined. Unless you have faith in the Light, you can not get close enough to perceive the Light. Father has never abandoned or even forsake, because inside you, you are the Father (ONE). How can you be separate from all that is when you are it? Look into the eyes of every man, woman, and child. You will see God, you will see creation. Yet, your ego perverts and destroys his image. Be brave enough to face one another. -Mother Theresa

Channeled by Craig
In service to all and the One

CHAPTER 4

My friends the Pleiadians and other Extraterrestrials

Note: Pleiades Star System, Distance from Earth 444.2 light years. Constellation: Taurus. Other names for the system include: M45, Seven Sisters, Melotte22

This is the part of my life in the upside down world of extraterrestrial visits, surgeries, abductions, and psychic telepathic communications. I don't even know where to start when it comes to telling you when and where or even how this all got started. But I will try my best to break it down in a somewhat sequential order. As my wife can attest to, I've been obsessed for many years now with reading book after book on E.T.'s and their interactions with humanity. The best and most helpful author I've discovered, is the late Delores Cannon who wrote such books as *The Custodians, Keepers of the Garden,* and *Legacy from the stars.* For without her books listing the hundreds of people interviewed under hypnosis and what they encountered with E.T.'s, I would feel truly lost.

For most people, any of this information may be well beyond your personal beliefs and may really test some of your religious dogma, too. One of the hardest things around all this phenomenon is the willingness for people to even share or try to explain the subject of E.T.'s to others. And for me, most of the time the information left behind is often too fragmented to make any sense of, let alone seem real. Again, what the hell is real anyway? There are so many layers and nuances that it's hard for an outsider to comprehend what contact is like and how it really affects a person. I can tell you from first hand experience that it is very psychologically rough on me. The psychic contacts are fun and interesting while the physical contacts are downright terrifying. The conscious mind has a terrible time trying to explain and quantify contact.

One of the most terrifying experiences I had was during the summer of 2018. I wrote down the experience shortly after so not to forget the most important details, as I often do. I think it's a subconscious defense mechanism, to protect my conscious mind. There is a lot of information around the contacts that I have received. They have come in both dribs and drabs over the years. Some were through conscious recall, through dreams, or what at least I thought were dreams. I've now done three hypnosis sessions in hopes of gaining a greater insight to this phenomenon as well. I highly recommend doing hypnosis if you suspect that you've had some interactions with or conscious visits from our E.T. neighbors.

7/12/18 Abduction event notes:

I became conscious that I was in a craft-UFO suspended in the air by both my wrists and ankles facing downward. The room was circular. Pretty sure I wasn't clothed either. I could see no visible restraints holding me in place. I was totally fucking terrified! There was a black-greyish looking E.T. behind me acting as an observer. There was a brown ugly E.T. in front of me who was the "doctor surgeon". Definitely not pretty, by any stretch of the imagination. It was a wrinkly brown humanoid alien with sparse dark hairs on its head. I can not define them as having a particular sex either. Their gender if even applicable, was not obvious to me.

I screamed and yelled at the Dr. E.T., - "Why are you doing this to me?"

His response was "Because you volunteered for this."

The first procedure was him sticking a large metal needle into the back right side of my jaw bone. The taste of metal in my mouth was heavy and intense. The second procedure was a long rod scoop device being inserted down my throat going into my stomach. This device then produced a black gooey ball that was extracted from the contents of my stomach. I asked what was the purpose of the operation? The reply was "to cure your diseases." Then at 3:05 am I found myself semi-conscious face down back in my bed crying. The pain in my stomach was awful and stayed with me for the next 24 hours.

At 3:20 am, the same moment I got up from bed, my dog in the next room got up, too. Maybe she sensed or was possibly aware of a problem with me. Elly greets me in the hall as tears run down my face. I go piss and then cry some more in the bathroom. In the next hour, I went three more times. At this point I was afraid to wake my wife. While she was still sleeping I placed my hand on her lower back trying desperately to gain some comfort as the night dragged into morning. I got no more sleep on that terrible night.

The next day I laid in bed until around 7:00 am. My wife came into the bedroom to inquire if I was going to work.

"No," I reply, "I'm taking a sick day."

She later inquired what was wrong with me, seeing my obviously distraught face.

"Was it a bad dream again?" she asked.

I lied and said yes so the story would be easier for her to digest. Later around 10:00 am after my daughter had gone off to camp, I went into my wife's home office and grabbed a chair to sit. I asked her to please be open minded, as this was not the first paranormal event to have occurred in our lives together. As an empathic individual, I hear, see, and feel all manner of psychic paranormal things. So for me to share something weird isn't out of the norm either. However this E.T. abduction event was by far the most out there.

So I was there sitting in my wife's office. I again asked her to keep an open mind. I then reiterated last nights events. Her whole demeanor shifted to an uncomfortable nervousness. Then she puts on a serious expression followed by a nervous laugh. In this moment she accepted my event as only a dream. Personally I get that you can't just ask a scientific analytical person to completely believe stories like that. What I found to be helpful afterwards was to have her listen to a previously recorded hypnosis session I had done a couple years prior. I think this gave more validity to my story. I can also speculate that people may put up psychological barriers so that they may not have to remember or experience these type of events at all. She questioned how I was even taken out of the house. I got the feeling there was some sort of Santa Clause vibe going on here. Later I invited her to look at the Einstein theory of what is a Rosen Bridge. Basically it is describing a wormhole, passing through one physical space to another physical space. That evening I was able to hook up with my teacher/healer. Physically I felt as if I was dragged down the stairs and hit every step on the way down. The session was a sort of rebirthing recall if I were to describe it, where I could review the whole event again. Here I was able to question them as to what was going on and find out more specifically as to what transpired. My teacher started off by asking what was going on since I had texted her at 4:00am in the morning. I then recounted the whole event to her in every detail. Then I climbed under the blankets on her massage table, a space of comfort and safety. Ten minutes or so went by when I was asked to put myself back into the moment of the abduction event. I then started to observe the event as a distant conscious observer.

My healer instructed me to ask my abductors questions. The first thing I asked was what was their purpose in taking me. They answered, "To cure diseases." Second question was why have they had chosen me? They told me I volunteered for this. Why was the needle stuck into the back of my jaw bone? They answered that they needed to remove cancer cells. And why was the device stuck down my throat? It was to remove stomach cancer. I had received a psychic message some months before this event that there was something growing in my stomach. Maybe I should pay more attention in the future.

After an hour or so on the healing table, my teacher suggested I should do a channeling when I got home. This would be to ask the E.T.'s that had abducted me for more details, if possible. What came through was even stranger to me than the event itself. My reality was about to be crushed.

Channeled after E.T. abduction surgery: 7/14/2018

Personal note from 7/14/18: I just had the biggest psychic breakthrough ever after doing a channel tonight. I tried to contact those who abducted me via channel. They replied with a flat out no, as they were too busy and were over by Australia working. Okay. So I thought what about the all black E.T. I had encountered in my yard one night many years back? I easily made contact and was very surprised as to what information came out of this communication.

Saturday Channel:

You've come back to meet yourself at several points in your own history now. In this very lifetime in fact. Be aware of how careful I or we had to be to accomplish this feat of time sequencing. This very activity is dangerous. And only a skilled tactician can accomplish this type of activity. Be it possible we will conspire to help one another now as we inhabit both bodies simultaneously. Incredible as this sounds the soul accomplishes this activity with slightly any effort. Your unconscious mind is aware. Just like in your dream activity you accomplish multiple parallel lives which you've already seen. Be careful in knowing this as we can not compete for the same identity. We will help each other through spontaneous remission of cancerous cells in your stomach and cheek bone area which were removed already this week. Eat your greens, that is an order.

Channeled By Craig

Time Stream Drawing: One morning I wok up with a vision of the art depicted here. I don't know how else to really describe it, other than I suspect it was downloaded to me overnight. I had to really marinate over it too, because it was so inexplicable. For months and months I was having what I thought was a dreamlike event of a trip aboard some sort of huge craft that was very hotel like on the inside. It was filled with people that

I cannot for the life of me remember. There were dozens of dreams/memories of being in a classroom setting there as well. The trip in and of itself sounds crazy enough, but the vision of the timeline was beyond anything I had encountered to date. This photo explanation from whatever life force gave it to me will test all your beliefs with regards to what is accepted in science and physics. From the E.T.'s: "This drawing was inserted to your matrix in order to explain your missing time and also for us to let you know the duration of your combined voyages; (total 4.5 years)." I found this information to be very disconcerting. How can I be missing that amount of time? Why hasn't it appeared to affect my age? I have many more questions surrounding all this. The time-stream drawing graphically depicts them removing me from my "perceived time line" and then returning me a very short time later via the confluence points. These points are like the doorways to plucking you out of dimensional reality and then reinserting you back in. However, while I was absent here, huge amounts of time had elapsed. This leaves me to conclude that humanity's perception of time is very relative and underdeveloped.

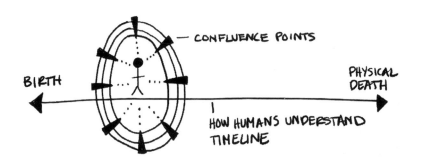

TIME STREAM EXPLAINED BY ETs

CONFLUENCE POINTS

BIRTH

PHYSICAL DEATH

HOW HUMANS UNDERSTAND TIMELINE

CHAPTER 5

Channels from the Pleiades

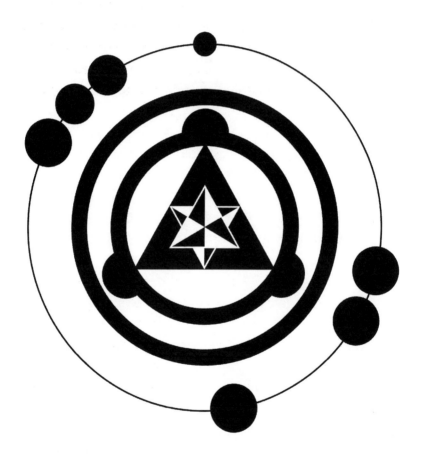

A Message of 2, part two

A light was broken when darkness was allowed to settle here on your planet Earth. She settled into a lower octave/density called 3rd density. This became a space where souls could once again experience polarity. Few stars are ever born without the cataclysm of energy. Imagine your souls as neutron star energy. The human body is but an appendage of the soul, a finger if you will. What we are trying to say is that your body is not in fact the center of the universe as you know it. The body is one of many attached to the soul having this life experience here on Earth. Think about that and digest it in thought, as everything is happening at once.
-The Pleiades

Channeled by Craig
In service to all and the One

Thinking small to think big

Come in closer. Let us see even yet closer into who you really are dear human race. DNA once again plays as a theme for your personal growth. An explosion arrives in it... into every molecule into your molecular growth. We must again address you on the level of the minutia. Looking into that thing which is barely ever seen, for your race, human being. Each molecule has its own nucleotide. Here at this precise point now to pinpoint activity, your growth begins. Not what you expected, but again it never is. Your building blocks are very complicated as we helped create this being your soul is now attached to. You hide its true purpose! Now an explosion of information is to arrive on Earth, and yet more light arrives each day. And now each cell in your DNA awakens little by little like a tiny voice calling out to each of you. Oh, it will just be a feeling. However it drives your madness into a self discovery. A dramatic affect it will have as the radiation kicks up... all while your planet slows down its rotation. The big clue here is in the magnetics. Like an engine it drives your DNA sequencing all at once. It is your choice to perceive it or not. Its effects will be seen everywhere. Look around at humanity's madness happening in your news and in your Earth as she erupts then quakes. You've been forewarned about this Fall season to come.. Those who choose to stay asleep will be swept up like the dirt into a dustpan. Are you conscious and aware? Have you thought this deeply yet? Pay much attention to this shift. All the little details matter at this time for your race.

-From the Pleiades a distant star family.

Channeled by Craig
In service to all and the One

The A.I. Mind Complex

A machine is to be built to serve all of humanity's needs. All are welcomed to choose what this mechanism has to offer. How will it appear? What is it that said machine will offer? I presume you all know this story and how it will end. It is Artificial Intelligence and it is not your friend. It's disruptive to the human cause. It is to be placed into the human brainstem and to help improve your intelligence. Its alternating current assumes your reality quadrant. It's presumed to help each and everyone who is choosing to use it. Even creating the miracle of allowing some of you to walk again and steering you clear of your dying breath. This is in fact what is to make you all "sheeple". Do not be fooled into a false reality when this technology emerges into your reality stream. It is said to be false; to be a trick into your own enslavement. If you're thinking that this sounds too fantastical... What would have George Washington thought of a cell phone? Could he have ever imagined? Be careful, and be warned.

-From the Pleiadian Agenda & High Council

Channeled by Craig
In service to all and the one

From The Pleiadian High Council

Greetings dearest ones. At your location in present day Earth we have greeted you many times, in many ways, and through many vessels such as Craig. This is your report card. We give each of you an A+. For even if you find yourself in the darkest of places; you are still serving your greatest purpose in being here. Here is now and now is here at the present moment. The past can't matter and the future you haven't met yet. Just be here in the present now.

You operate in a narrative that is sometimes devoid of hope. Why you ask? Not to be punished, for you are all perfect in our eyes. The mission is for you to succeed and after countless lifetimes raise your vibrational frequency to one of love, one of soul purpose. Good bad or otherwise you are each serving your greatest purpose in doing that which it is that you do. Just be in the moment. Sit with who you are. Listen to your soul expression. Hear your soul speak.

You've had to descend to a much lower vibrational frequency to learn about your own emotionality. Through this roller coaster of emotion you both learn and grow. Be impressed with yourselves. This journey is not easy, for you have had to forget who you are and where it is you came from. Be blessed. -The Pleiades

Channeled by Craig
In service to all and the One

Not sleeping anymore..

A Promise has been kept for humanity's sake. We have intermittently shared information with those who are like family to us. Periodically we request that these humans share words on our behalf. A time comes closer when we'll all be in contact with one another again. Those who are here as "sleepers" will hear the bell toll and be called into service like pieces on the chess board. It's time you heard your true calling, sleepers. Open your eyes to the skies, look towards the heavens. That blinking light and those goosebumps running down your arms, that sense that someone is there with you but not. No! You are never alone nor have you been forgotten, star-seeds. Your soul's choice was a delayed opening to this game. Now the spark is being ignited so you may come to realize that you are, or may be, something else entirely. "The sleepers must awaken."

Channelled by Craig
In service to all and the One

Inspiration is in everything

Few words differentiate the actuated value of time and of the space sub-continuum. The actual particle matter of space is split between the difference of a subatomic particle. This ratio is then subdivided by zero time. The cold space between planets can be encountered by this living breathing matter, for it is all alive. The fabric of space time holds copious amounts of subatomic energy. So in actuality you exist in time and space simultaneously. As you live and breath so does the universe, coinciding with the matter inside your body. For all is One.

This description to us is like for you humans to say an apple is red. We understand this as simple fact. We think it and it will evolve into happening. For us to travel to a far off star planet; it is as if you were to hold a piece of paper, then fold it in half and then poke a hole through its center. You can coincide at two places at once. From here to there is a short distance. You can exist outside of time and matter, living without age. Energy will never cease to exist or die, but rather it will simply change form. Your intuition is your guide into the folds of spacetime. The "clock" does not exist here. All is now, nothing else. Be delighted in who you really are dearest humans, for we are the Pleiades.

Channeled by Craig
In service to all and the One

What is the Matrix?

The physical construct of the universe is ever changing. This is due in part to the sun in your immediate solar universe, as we would call it. In your neighborhood the immediate dynamic creates its very own dichotomy. Meaning you are what you see as so you are just plain frequency. So, should you use your freewill to just simply shift by turning the metaphorical dial. This takes stature and mental fortitude on your part personally. Your spark has its own resonance (zip code). Each spark acts like its own microchip on your computer motherboard. Your frequency is much more multidimensional than you can ever imagine. Never before has this been explained in quite this way. You are in control! The dark force assumes it has contained enough mass to keep you enslaved. Rest assured the quickest way out of this proverbial "soup" is to move up in frequency.

But how do I do that you ask? Change your diet. Quite literally everything you consume spiritually, emotionally, physically, and yes sexually changes who and what you are. Does the news media pollute your consciousness? Yes, in every possible way. You only think that you believe in the right political party. There is no right side, as it's simply now a control devise to keep you all mentally corralled like sheep. Are you sheep? The only direction and voice you should ever listen to is your inner light. Light is to its own frequency as is the dark as well. Those in servitude to the dark harness all the worst aspects of this creator power, such as lust, greed, guilt, and other influences of the dark matrix. And so in light of seeing the world filled with turmoil, please know that you have the option to reject this reality. When you say "that's it, no more" the world will start to shift and the dark will lose its control of your frequency matrix.

-The Pleiades

Channeled by Craig
In service to all and the One

Black Hole Sun 9/11

A coming forth of new and relevant information here... stay tuned as your news people like to say. Words don't just happen to fall onto your page here. We're here with purpose to help humanity's cause. But will you listen? We believe you will. Now let's begin in cooperation. The Sun hole is in question, noted by the 9/11 date on your calendar year. Take notice of the magnetic changes that will occur on the earth now with your corresponding DNA changes happening too. One thing affects the other, a cause and effect. You'll notice energy changes in frequency occurring. It is a ripple effect... like dropping a large stone into a body of water. This Sun portal opened to let through a new magnetic wave into your solar system and it was by universal intention to make changes into your DNA pool. Be prepared for it, it too will wreak havoc on the uninitiated. If you haven't done your work yet, it will be like orchestra symbols being clapped into your ears. How loud will this affect sing/ring? We watch in great anticipation. We are the Pleiades.

Channeled by Craig
In service to all and the One

From me to them for us

To begin once again, hello we are the Pleiades. Not sure if we mentioned this before as we're speaking through Craig who is our messenger and universal conduit. As a receiver he is asked a lot to convey our messages for reasons yet unknown to himself. Sacrifice had to be given on his part to clear the way through his heart in order to convey our messages and directive if you will. Not all of this is shiny and roses for him. He has had to bear this as a burden as well; in that he's been pressed to change in many ways that he could not have conceived. Our property and our manifest is in his DNA. A progeny of alien DNA if you will and a volunteer soul from our side of the universe. 350 lifetimes he's lived among you, fighting wars, experiencing holocausts, and facing great perils along his soul's journey here. And it has been his honor to be the ancestry of Enoch, bringer of the Christ consciousness here on Earth. It is time we share in a deeper way through this conduit. It is also time that greater light is brought out through all our soldiers of light here on planet earth. It is our intent to win and beat the powers of darkness from the inside, through such vessels as yourselves (humans). We're ready to begin our assault in a non-violent way to make humanity stand and take notice... it is on your shoulders to win here, not ours, as it is our directive to be non-interference.

Channeled by Craig
In service to all and the One

If you'd stop and listen

What is it we're asking of humanity? Again this comes with much concern for your human species. Don't look up expecting to be saved. Save yourselves! This is your opportunity to learn, not ours... as observers we learn a lot here though. Again, we are so concerned as we now explore options on how exactly to help with us being "non-interference". So what to begin with? Most obviously yourselves. Unplug from the system which constantly distracts and controls your attention. And while you're watching the fire tornado this week; there are those whom are reaching into your pockets, looking at your personal background and data, loading the next injection of poison to sell you.

At this point we are saying rather than asking who are your masters? Whom are their masters... the dark ones... the so called overlords feeding off your physical energetic negativity. All the while keeping you weak, it is their sole purpose. We're calling you out! As they breath in your toxic energy, be awoken to the thought that they control your species until you decide to break free. The perfect point to start at is closing your eyes and hearing your true inner voice, not the TV. The one begging to be saved. Humanity are you listening? Wake up.
-from the Pleiades.

Channeled by Craig
In service to all and the One

Thought Creation

A chemical molecule is an atomic particle stretching out across the universe in every direction. To give physical matter to all things created equally by the ONE. It is a matter of purpose for the universe to create like this. A star's birth is a collision of energies and platelets of reality collapsing in on themselves, this then creating a sort of sub-atomic particle if you will. The purpose in all this is greater than we can express at this very moment in channel. However, we do want to express sincere gratitude to those who listen to each and every channel written by Craig.

Channeling is an innate ability for all humans who wish to create something out of thin air. A division occurs in your spirit while channeling. A part of the ego gets turned off while the higher mind comes in as a sort of conduit. Perception varies from person to person and each soul has a distinct voice and a willingness to be heard. Now do you get up each day in drudgery or are you inspired to enrich one another? Be aware that you are what you think and as you think so shall you create. Be safe and be well. We are the Pleiades.

Channeled by Craig
In service to all and the One

A message for the Star Seeds

A positive message from your beginning. A note worthy of listening to your past experiences here for Earth. A possible conclusion for a moment's rest. Today we begin to tell your story from the start of the creation point. A "seed" was planted here on Earth within your species. The hope was to evolve you enough to take your species back to your creation point. Why you ask? Not that your species would be the first one but rather the most emotionally evolved one. Not one other species possesses your range of emotions. It's what allows you to experience light and dark the way you do here. It is what allows you to feel things that others can't. This is why visitors are here... chasing evolutionary cause on their own behalves. Not to say that others aren't here to help you because they in fact are. It's just many agendas exist under this umbrella. Be prepared to help as they are listening and desire your soul's cooperation. Each of these other species (originally 28 in your DNA pool) dropped off souls here with hidden agendas. Mostly hidden from the conscious minds of humans they exist into or inhabit. Each serving its own cause and evolutionary process. Ascension is the bridge for you and them, humanity. This is the wave in which other species want to follow and evolve by. It is the road back to Source. The hand of God if you will. This is why they come... this is why they visit so many here. It is because you are them and they are you. One does not get to evolve without helping the other... a cause and effect symbiosis.

Channeled by Craig
In service to all and the One

May 30th 2018 channel

From The Pleiades: It is time once again for your species to learn. Who this channel is isn't important so much as what you know now. 9th dimensional reality comes into play in this conversation. Now start to imagine a new paradigm! A beginning point where you can no longer stand in your past. Forward is the only option and direction for those who channel and carry light in their hearts dear Light Workers. No more can we or you accept the current negative paradigm. It just doesn't work anymore for your new beginning taking place here. Now welcome in the 12th density of an even higher energy. Its emergence carries with it an infinite possibility, where you can now create your very own fabric of reality (be your own creator). Lets stop here for today before going any further. Step back, take a peaceful breath, please remember you are the Light Workers, the voice of God.

Channeled by Craig
In service to all and the One

June 1ˢᵗ 2018 channel

From the Pleiades:
This transmission begins in hope of you now stepping forward into who you really are!! We are so excited to bring new news to Earth Gaia in hopes of retrieving what was lost eons ago due to the chaos on your planet. We now begin to once again raise the vibration of the planetary grid, so lost ruins will rise again, metaphorically speaking. It is in your chronological genomes, where we aim to draw your attention to now. Your ancestry was never truly lost when the Pleiadians left this earth or even when the darkness collapsed your mythical Atlantis. But be certain it was real. You too have this underlying feeling now? This hope, this gratitude that real change will take place this

time around on the 4th Earth. Success is imminent when you all collectively hold light in your hearts. So be prepared for great changes to take place! The light is on and we want you all to now see.

Channeled by Craig
In service to all and the One

June 21st 2018 Channel

So a few words here about humanity's story: It is us the Pleiadians again, in so far as we are able to transmit at a distance to the vessel's mind so it is channeled to paper. Let us begin again. Thus it is important to recognize what is humanities position in the universe. And, it goes without saying that it is much less advanced than it should be at this point in its current history, and for its current timeline. Yes, there are two stories occurring here at once. One is being told through Craig with pen and paper, the other is through humanity's TV broadcasting, through which you are being manipulated too. Obvious sarcasm through us here, but the point is well made. Each image you're being shown on the TV has an affect on your mental status and also your conscious thought pattern. Pictures of inhumanity disturb your mind for weeks and months long after you see them. So let us then consider that you are being programmed at a rate never before imagined. Are you being programmed for good? Obviously not. Just some food for thought. You are what you consume most. If the images are of horror, then your life has an underlying energy of horror. It is that simple, just like with food laden with chemicals you've chosen to eat. Add all that up and you have a dumbed down spiritually dead human. So wake up! Eat and consume that of which you feel Love for. Do yourselves a favor, start your own plants, garden or what have you, heal your planet Gaia, the place you call home.

Channeled by Craig
In service to all and the One

June 24ᵗʰ 2018
Channeled from the Pleiades

Always we are to begin by seeing the "creator" as a whole, as a One, a singularity. It is an infinite and also finite possibility existing everywhere at once. Flowing through us all in a current of electrical pulse. This is our effort to describe the I AM: The God presence in everyone everywhere, each existence, each creation; touched by the One creator. God resonates in everyone. However you were taught to believe something entirely different. Wake up child in man, become who you really are. We are all touched by the creative hand that drives this universe. Welcome as we are in the infinite, the call to join source. We are beckoned by this call deep inside of everyone. Creator at its source is but one singularity, one possibility, one hope, one wish, one beginning that has been split into an infinite amount of possibilities. So let us begin by stating once again, "Greetings humanity!" We are in your presence through Craig; we reach out through source to touch your inner space that hasn't been identified yet, but will soon be. Soon it will become your beckoning call to look inside of yourselves, to close your eyes and see within, to know infinite possibility again. Hear us, as we whisper your name. Angels calling from far away places. Do not be disturbed. Like others we've watched and observed your creation come into being, God's touch if you will. We say hello. Have you answered back humanity? So have you?

Channeled by Craig
In service to all and the One

It is just stardust

The diasporic universe will collapse in upon itself. What does this mean for your humanity? Nothing, if you do not believe in ONE. All affects all, all is in everything, even the smallest spec of dust. All are made from the same fractals that are the building blocks of the universe, just like your DNA. Picture your DNA now as a 3D model spinning clockwise, moving in perfect sequence. For you to understand this analogy we must now use the most extreme example. Humans fight and attack one another in made up dramas called war. If you were to elevate your consciousness high enough, you would begin to see and then recognize the DNA anatomy in one another. Once you see that you all are made of the same stuff, you would know without a doubt that you were in fact ONE. So how does that sound? The building blocks of life are fractals. It's all just sacred geometry. Amen.
-The Aetri, distant E.T. brothers and sisters

Channeled by Craig
In service to all and the One

Note: This channel was done after I made an initial contact with them (the Aetri) during my spiritual development class. This was while we were trying to read info off of a piece of moldavite asteroid rock. Their galaxy location is the Milky Way. Alternate names include Alpha Trianguli Australis, Alf Tra, HD 150798, HIP 82273, HR 6217. Located at a distance of light years 390.61 from Earth

From The Aetri to me

We are back in communication here with you now to describe another planet that you did not know about yet, hidden in the star Nebula of Atris. Hidden away on the outskirts of another universe, this is our water world. We are all sea creatures as you humans like to say in your earth language. And, what we appear to resemble most closely is your Orca, killer whales. However we are anything but what you are thinking of in this distant communication today. You too, Craig had once spent a lifetime of about a hundred years or so here on this planet. This concept may be difficult for you to conceive of given what your current embodiment looks like (humanoid). But be assured that you did spend time with us on the water world. Deep thoughts will arise after this communication today. You'll begin to evolve in a different way, not just through your DNA, but your sight, taste, touch, and smell senses will change. A dampening will occur to buffer your senses which are emotionally too hard to handle at times. Being once of this water world makes you an intensely emotional person. This is no mistake. You may feel this at a further distance than anyone else around you. How else do you think you were able to reach us from so far away? The distance is too vast for others to connect here in a psychic

way in which you have done today. This water world you may call home and you are always welcome back. Swim with us some more.
-The Aetri.

Channeled by Craig
In service to all and the One

Channeled from the Pleiades, Life 101

So a lesson to say the least, is that humanity against its will is quickly approaching a paradigm shift (meaning some of you are fighting this). The reason is plain and simple: you are ready to emerge from your shadows or rather your shadow of self. What is it in yourself which you do not like? Look in the mirror and acknowledge this self, your darker self. Own it as it is going to need to be worked through and incorporated back into the higher self aspect of your being. Not until you resolve this shadow self... There is no escalator waiting to take you to the next level so to speak. But we are here to let you know now that it is ready to be approached. So own it! And congratulate it, for it made you who you now are. Your struggles are all recognized through the higher self of your being. It is in its stage of growth to where it must now reach down and acknowledge its darker component... the yin and yang of your somewhat hidden selves. Enjoy who you are, be who you are, no more masks are needed. Your true selves shall emerge.

Channeled by Craig
In service to all and to the One

2:30am channel

In our words, you've come too far to look back anymore. There is only the future at this point in your existence. Forget about the so called Karma and trouble of your youths. Lets now build a new bridge of hope together. This is the Pleiades and we're from your future point in time where you will quantum leap into your very own existence in the next 300 years. In order to get there you must first awaken to the idea that we are all One and realize your God selves and individual potential as well. One is all and all is One. Be blessed on your way through this journey as it is going to get rough now. However now you've chosen to have this, this very way. The sun shines down on new ideas where you look inwards in order to explore the known universe, the micro of the macro as you like to say in your economic terms. Be well and be on your way journey seekers. -We are the Pleiades.

Channeled by Craig
In service to all and to the One

CHAPTER 6

The Mantid Connection

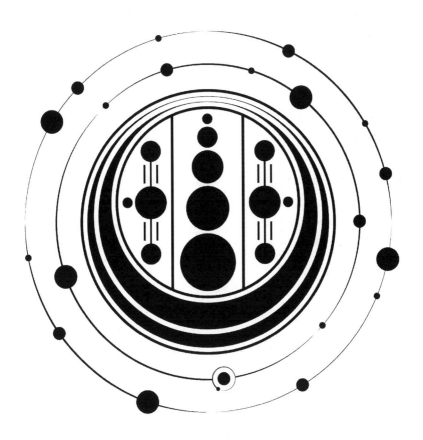

Interview (channeling) with a Mantid: From contact with my associate whom I call Dr. Drex

Appearance: Yes, you guessed it, they look like a praying mantis.

General overview: Their population may be both expanded and collapsed depending on what is needed for their society to develop and current resources available. They each can have many children, birthed via eggs. The mother is responsible for rearing entirely. They are very science based and all of Earth's great scientists may have interacted with their energies. Demeanor is very calm and logical, not a great range of emotion, making them perfectly suited for being the conductors of operations involving other E.T.'s (joint ventures).

The following points were stated by Drex, and as he stated, the issues which were most pressing to his agenda. I came to know him through receiving repair work after doing a channel for Einstein. The energy was way too much for me to handle at the time and very, very expansive. I can only bring through what I can handle. I had Drex return once more after Tesla came through via channel. That night after the Tesla channel, it was a night of very restless sleep for me. In fact I was waking my wife up speaking in another language of which she could not recognize. My guides said its origin was that of Alpha Centauri. Since these interactions with Drex, we've been able to have some telepathic conversations with one another and they were very fascinating to me.

1. The holocaust was not allowed to happen but was rather forced to happen by dark E.T.'s; we'll call them reptilian. Not all are bad however, as some reside on the side of light now, though their numbers are very few. The dark ones are ingrained here much like a tick riding on its host's back, draining mana. They are feeding on an ooze-like substance generated by your negativity. Be appreciative of your reality as it requires great bravery to be here in this lower vibrational existence.

2. Who we are: We are the energy engineers sent here to fix and restore value and rebalance the system of polluted energies. We're still cleaning up and restoring energies from the holocaust. This energy is like a stain and is imprinted into your time sequence.

3. The War: Just like so many other races are, we too are sending souls here now in the present moment to be implanted/incarnated so to speak within the human race. This is how we're affecting change and winning the war on the "Dark" upon the Earth right now. Taking on the battle from the inside. This is our generational involvement, sending those souls who are not corruptible.

4. Dimensional rift: A degree of separation in and of self occurs as the divide between light and dark happens. Be prepared to see things disappear and then reappear, (time loopholes). The effect is like you squinting while looking at the sun, and then looking away from the brightness while next trying to refocus to quickly.

5. Human development: What we hope to learn through interacting with your species is purely for emotional gain. Not many species have your emotional range. This is what excites us and makes you all so unpredictable. Sequencing in your DNA is now starting to unravel. Be prepared to look inside with wonder and amazement, to see your hidden potential.

6. NASA Black Ops: Most importantly it has been noted by us that your government's newer technologies are being deployed by the secret space program. These technologies have been hidden from your race. The illusion is in your control matrix. The unbelievable is more real than you can possibly imagine. It is your combined collective consciousness that frees your race. So decide if you want war or peace. Peace brings great prosperity to all here on earth. Are you listening?

7. How You See: A collision of realities is occurring right now as we speak. Stop thinking in 3D. Your perception is too narrowed by thinking in this way. Open your eyes, all of them. Through practiced meditation this will naturally occur for you all.

8. Hand In Hand: Building our future together will for now remain only a distant possibility. If you want our help just ask. We're working behind the scenes ever so diligently on your behalf.

Drex follows up by saying that I too carry part of your DNA strand and so does the Master Builder race (the stone people). They may harbor resentment for your species, however after dealing with your shadow government faction, be warned.

CHAPTER 7

Everybody in the pool

A Place in Time

In other words I will take that which is mine. Does this sound familiar? I know it does for a lot of you. The cause is certain as it rings true for so many. Many divisions exist within your society at this point in time. This is by design, do not be mistaken, and not too complicated I must say. I too was such an architect with many bad hypocritical things to say, as I myself was a Jew. Though however, I persecuted and did the most unspeakable of things.

Here and now I must explain what it is to be called the soul agreement. And I state that one's soul gathered back at Source (God) isn't any more bad or good than any another. I repeat, this life experience is God experiencing itself. So do not make it all about you. You will all take turns here being both the villain and the hero. This is so humanity may learn what is needed in the next step to its evolution. Be warned however, this time in front of you now is a test of true faith. Many things

will come to pass and you must now choose which side of history you are to be on. I have atoned for my sins at Source. God's forgiveness is for all his children. Be blessed.
- Adolph Hitler

Channeled by Craig
In service to all and the One

North or South

A few little words so that I might share a great secret with all humans today. This is Sheila, a clairsentient being from what is to be described as middle Earth. Great secrets are kept within the Earths magnetosphere. In your news we have alerted you all to the seismic shifts. These are ripples running across Gaia's skin. It is just like as if you were to get a chill when a spirit walks up on you. Now imagine God walking up on Gaia and whispering in her ear. Great changes are coming for you great mother. North will be south and south will be north, so shall the east be west. Oneness and the Unity has commanded this great change to occur. So shake those fleas from your back as I call the unwanted souls back home to source. These souls are to be re-assigned elsewhere in the universe. They will be put to work teaching the unity of light and dark. So do not fret when large tracts of humans are swept away in the waves of shaking which are to now occur.

All who are to stay, be prepared, for it is you who will own this day. Some may accelerate up and past this event and never suffer at God's right hand. Others who stay, will face their own darkness. 3D is to be left behind, but not forgotten on the old

earth. The split shall seem as if seamless, as if nothing occurred at all. And now in that, let you worry about you. This is your souls journey. It will all be worked out as planned, amen.
-Sheila

Channeled by Craig
In service to all and the One

A channel from Cowoost Earth Elder of Ancient Earth II

The turn of the next century will be revered. As to why is yet to be discovered by you dear humans. Free energy in part, will free you from the slavery of oil. Suppression of knowledge will dissolve. New thoughts and ideas will evolve too. A single thought, a single action by a species such as yours will give rise to yet a new evolutionary process. The rest of the communities in your solar universe will sit up and take notice. This happens once the wave crashes and the water draws back into your oceans. A people such as yourselves will realize the punishment of such selfish actions were brought upon by yourselves. Awaken to an inner voice and listen to where you need to be star seeds.t Mother Earth awaits your kindness and new ideas for her future.

Channeled by Craig
In service to all and the One

Good bedfellows

A timetable of a parable is no exception when it comes to thought creation. Never be jealous of others in so much as to say that those who have more than you are better. Those that are the poorest respectfully to God are the most humble and appreciative. They've chosen the simpler and yet harder foot path to find a way back to creator. They were not the selfish or thoughtless when they had arrived back here in the embodiment of man.

I often read letters from those appealing to our higher good senses. And yet higher wisdom did prevail allowing us to turn a cornerstone in our nation's history book. There are those who fought to take advantage of what we had created in our newly birthed nation. However, we did stop them at that time. They've remained with a strong foothold. You call them the Illuminati, we called them the unjust. They kept the gold bullion for themselves. Why? You can't eat it and you cant take it with you when you die. This gold was stolen from the Inca's and had been traded many times over moving hand to hand. It stunk of a lust for power, a dark corruption. You see me as a Mason and wonder what was my involvement in this plot. I was just a mere player in the game and strongly desired recognition of right and nobility.

A great player now leads this country which I no longer recognize. No doubt he too wants recognition. He does not desire or need money at this point, it's all for soul accomplishment. Go back in time and you can see the ascension and escalation to his great power. However, the wall he's created and the political strife will be his only remembrance. What flies in the face of dishonest men, lies within their heart's good graces. Be well and do not be forgotten in your own legacy.

-President Washington

Channeled by Craig
In service to all and the One

The many hands of God

There are many obstacles which can and shall be removed from one's own existence while you are in this human form. As there are struggles that each and every one of us has to face. How we face the daily life, is of much importance to the soul in our existence here. Worry not as each of these things can and shall be overcome, much like climbing a wall covered in vines.

The words you use each and every day carry both thought and meaning. So be mindful as to what it is you speak. Each word is a projection out into the world. Words carry much meaning, as do they carry a message as well. Make sure to use kindness while speaking your words, take ownership of them. I Ganesha have thought to say these words for quite some time now. And now in this time it makes perfect sense for to me to do so. Kindness is your fellowship duty towards the common man, for you should treat all others as your equal. Find kindness in everything you do and do not sway from this intention. For if you are to speak ill words, you will have to halt your development and step backwards.

An even swell exists now in the infinite energy crossing the known universe. Your sun acts as its catalyst too. So do not

despair when you see chaos and disorder. This is the universe trying to set each thing right. The creator seeks balance in all of its aspects, for there can be no greater harmony than the life pulse of the creator, for you are all now infinite and expansive energies of the source creator. Be joyed, be happy, and be well.
-Ganesha

Channeled by Craig
In service to all and the One

Sun Spots

So much new information is coming at you now, that it can often be overwhelming. Much the same way that humanity is to start receiving a DNA upgrade through the full spectrum of the sun's light frequency. Others will worry that the sun's dormancy is now an issue here. This is not at all your concern, for this portal you call the sun is pausing to recalibrate your message. This change is massive in frequency disruption for the human race. For the sun must work through your frequency disruptors, like for example the cell towers and phones harming your DNA. This has also been evident in your poisons like DDT. Also, look at the honey bees disappearing. This is humanity's canary in the coal mine moment. What is your legacy? What is it you are leaving behind? Is it a planet of pollution and oceans of garbage? Be not wasteful dearest humans. Be good stewards to the Earth.
-from Earth Elder Spirit Steve.

Channeled by Craig
In service to all and the One

Face to face with one's self

Construction of self is the most important issue for us all... how we individually build ourselves, the identity we create based around the wounds we take in as children. Visualize yourselves going in and meeting the childlike self. This meeting will be your first time encounter with the child self. Ask what it is this child needs? To whom does it respond and maybe even fear? Capitalize on this very moment. Extend your hand to the child, so you may embrace it. Take a moment to both love and share. What is it you hear from your inner child? What is the request? Is it to be loved, feared, hated, or a feeling of jealousy that needs your attention? These issues we all contain and absorb on the journey into adulthood. Humanism is who we are. Glorious are the opportunities to actually perhaps face our deepest selves. The reflection you all see in the mirror is just a mirage. A construct built around who you think you are in this 3D matrix reality. The more we face and own our true selves, the more we can be who we truly are.
-Sheila, planet historian

Channeled by Craig
In service to all and the One

Channeled from: Cowoost, Earth Elder of the Earth Gaia

A story begins again to unfold for humanity. Very much the same message as yesterday's channel, but I as in One offer a twist never before heard by this channel's ears. That is one brought about by a volcano. It brings down humanity into the deepest desperation and despair. ("You're saying this beginning is an ending for us?") Not exactly, but a starting point to recover your humanity. ("What is the meaning of this?") You will begin to prosper again when the eruption flows and wipes its feet at humanity's doorstep. To say no further action is needed is impossible. You'll be crushed by natures defeating purpose. New times offer new changes though. An opportunity to unplug from the grid holding humanity captive. New thought and new emotions that arise like that within the Earth's crust. Then a wave crashes and silence will be heard around the planet all at once. Ancient "god" Sumerian Karma finally comes home to roost. The changes that were made to humanity's DNA matrix left you incomplete. But this was on purpose and their ancestry is in all your ruling elite today, the kings and queens, even your Trump. Whether he realizes that or not is another story entirely. Be calm now, be fulfilled with your own happiness inside, unplug yourself from this ruling elite. They cast a strong shadow. But internal light can not be put out. Amen.

Channeled by Craig
In service to all and the one

From 4th to 5th Earth

Greetings, I am Cowoost, former inhabitant of your planet earth and now guardian soul. I am here for all those in need of help during the great transition. This will be a most tumultuous time for sure. Some will wonder is it an apocalypse or a second coming of the Christed one? Neither is my pronounced answer to your query. But a new home is being made now for each of you who is ready to arrive in what is called 5th Earth or the 5th dimensional reality.

The old souls are here now and are to anchor in the new energies during this transition period. They may not be physically old, please remember that. Great wisdom will come from the youngest of children even. Now perhaps it is an opportunity for you to all adjust and drop your masks and finally let ego die once and for all. This new reality happens in the present moment and it's all how you choose to create it through your God self. Each one of you is an aspect of creator, a part of divinity. It's time you recognized this. Be well dear ancestors for a great journey awaits you, again.
-Cowoost

Channeled by Craig
In service to all and the One

Father Bear Elk

A star, a neutron, an atom. Whispers are heard in all these things. And it is your story of creation too. Plato arrived at this very conclusion, as did others before him. I am Chieftain Odawa of Black Bird Canyon. My forefathers came from Lemuria and first stepped foot onto this continent you call the US. It was never yours to take but was ours to mother and care for with respect. Now it is time for the trade winds to shift. Others under a red flag will want to take what you perceive as being yours. Tears run long down my aged face as I can see and anticipate great struggles coming to your country called the U.S.. Be aware that life is a gift not to be squandered away on any level. For now the rivers run deep but for someday they

Please welcome us back to your planet, not as antagonists but as energy evolvers. Create a new thinking of that which is beyond yourselves. Be imaginative, it is the new seed of hope for the Sun Children being born now into this next generation. They are the builders and architects of a new dimensionality for your planet. They see well beyond 3D. They are your reclaimers. Be prepared for your new children who are sent here to be masters!

-Quetzalcoatl

Channeled by Craig
In service to all and the One

Migrants and the Matrix

A bridge must be crossed for humanity to obtain its own freedom here on earth. You are not free, not in a system like this. Countless lives are being eaten up by a system that systematically destroys individuated lives, for the sole purpose of personal gain and self interest.

A bridge must be crossed in order for you, dear humans, to actually meet one another for the first time. Do you think you have actually really authentically met one another? No, as it is our truth to explain here that you rest your eyes of judgement wearily upon one another. There within you, you have feelings of greed, fear, personal gain, prejudice and envy.

Why now must you cross this bridge? Let us explain once and for all. Unless you start helping those in need and treating all others as your equal; you've achieved exactly nothing. It is the ultimate spiritual goal for this humanity to recognize that you are all ONE. You all come from the same Source. You are individuated sparks sent out into the universe by Creator, so to be the faculty of God's own creation reflecting back in upon itself.

Be realized in who you are now recognizing and acknowledging the God self. Nothing is separate, though in your perceived reality it does appear to be that way. This is your mirror, it is all around you. Look into the eyes of one another and see your own reflection. There is only you.

-from Cowoost Earth Elder

Channeled by Craig
In service to all and the One

CHAPTER 9

Perspective

You may be wondering, what my perspective on life is now that I've shared all these messages with you? I have had to change a lot of my negative perceptions about the world. That has been the most challenging for me, to not be so opinionated. I fight with that side of myself all the time. I feel a split between the spiritual self and the day to day self that gets up and goes to work each moening. When I step into the 9 to 5 office world, I have to put on my normalcy mask. Then when I sit down to channel, I get to be the "real" me, the side I love, the side I wish I could be all the time. But for many of us who are tapped into the other side, this can be a big challenge. It is just a matter of fact that not all the people around us are ready to look behind the curtain. But when they do, we will be waiting to help them take the next step in evolution.

Many experiences through healing, dreaming, and meditation have altered my being slowly over time. Some of the star-seed, E.T. experiences, are in my mind like scars that cannot be erased. These are the things I just cannot unsee. The multi-dimensional world of E.T.'s and alternate dimensions is not just black and white. I find that it is rather something I must think about daily, as it is so deeply ingrained in my psyche. Experiences as far back as twenty plus years ago will still come up and catch me off guard, too. The upside is that I get to process them a little more each time and make new connections on who these beings are and how exactly it is that they relate to me. There are layers of information in some of the simplest of experiences and interactions. There are no coincidences around these events.

After I had taken my La Ho Chi (healing modality) training, I somehow instinctively knew that I could astral project myself out into the edge of space. I have no idea why I had such an inclination. But the experience will never leave me. During the OBE, I looked back at the solar systems while being immersed into the blackness of space. The space where I found myself was full of sound. It was a static noise-filled environment, with its vibrations and clicks. This is what brought me to the understanding that the universe was very much alive and breathing. This was me meeting the ONE. Some experiences will cause you to forget everything you ever knew as true and change your perspective completely. This life changing paradigm shift taught me to never think of things in the absolute, because nothing is absolute.

Epilogue

If you have read your way through all of the channeled messages in this book, I thank you for indulging in my work. It has been my highest honor to complete this project. The past year and a half has been the most interesting journey of self discovery. Now the end result is this book. My hope is this is just the beginning because I have enjoyed the experience so much. I find it rewarding, and often feel elated after finishing a channel while being up late at night.

You may already be familiar with some of the subject matter that has been presented in this book, and now even more so after reading my channels. There is a great deal of similar information on the internet and from other channelers. But I want you to understand there is no one real absolute source of information; and that enlightenment unfolds across many fields of reality. These realities and time threads are ever changing as we migrate through 4D existence. My objective is to get people to think well beyond what is in the scope of their everyday normal perceptions. There is so much we don't yet understand about our universe. Mankind too is unfolding and moving from this dense perception of life to a much lighter essence of being. This is why the darkness and horrors of the world are so in your face right now. We each need to look at ourselves in the mirror and own our dark aspect in order to balance out this polarity. This will enable each of us to reclaim our light. Only then will we be able to graduate to the next level of existence on this human journey.

REFERENCES

Cannon, D. *The custodians "Beyond Abduction"* Huntsville AR: Ozark Mountain Publishers, 1999.

Cannon, D. *Legacy From The Stars* Huntsville AR: Ozark Mountain Publishers, 1996.

Cannon, D. *Keepers Of The garden* Huntsville AR: Ozark Mountain Publishers, 1993.

Pleiades, Wikipedia contributors, 26 January 2019 https://en.wikipedia.org/w/index.php?title=Pleiades&oldid=880256898 ID: 880256898

Alpha Trianguli Australis, Wikipedia contributors, 29 January 2019, https://en.wikipedia.org/w/index.php?title=Alpha_Trianguli_Australis&oldid=880858871 ID: 880858871

Notes

_____

_____

_____

_____

_____

_____

_____

_____

_____

_____

_____

_____

_____

_____

_____

_____

_____

_____

_____

Notes

_____

_____

_____

_____

_____

_____

_____

_____

_____

_____

_____

_____

_____

_____

_____

_____

_____

Made in the USA
Middletown, DE
02 June 2019